Original title:
Into the Unknown

Copyright © 2024 Creative Arts Management OÜ
All rights reserved.

Author: Cassandra Whitaker
ISBN HARDBACK: 978-9916-88-892-6
ISBN PAPERBACK: 978-9916-88-893-3

Where Possibility Meets Mystery

In shadows dance the dreams, so bright,
Unfurling wings in the quiet night.
Paths unknown call out with soft allure,
Where hopes and fears find a thread that's pure.

Tangled thoughts spin webs of chance,
In silent corners, the heart's romance.
Fleeting moments, oh so rare,
Merge the known with the open air.

The Voyage to Unfathomed Realms.

With compass set towards the unknown,
We sail on seas of dreams overblown.
Stars above, like lanterns, lead,
Guiding us through the waves, we heed.

Each wave whispers secrets lost at sea,
In currents deep, we seek to be free.
Together we venture, hand in hand,
Creating tales of a far-off land.

Beyond the Veil of Certainty

Lifting the veil, what lies beyond?
A world where thoughts and shadows bond.
In twilight's grip, we dare to dream,
Finding light in the softest gleam.

Questions linger in the stillness there,
Echoing whispers that float in air.
Truth dances just out of touch,
In spaces crafted with love as such.

Whispers of the Uncharted

As winds carry tales of distant shores,
In every breath, the wanderer pours.
Hidden valleys and ancient trees,
Sing songs of adventure upon the breeze.

In twilight's glow, we trace the map,
Of whispers hushed in nature's lap.
With every step, the heart reveals,
The magic woven into our heels.

The Enigma of Tomorrow

Whispers of dawn dance on the breeze,
Shadows of doubt drift with ease.
Hope flickers like a candle's glow,
Tomorrow's promise, we do not know.

Stars linger in the velvet night,
Guiding dreams with silver light.
Each choice a step on the winding way,
The enigma deepens with each new day.

Steps into the Abyss

Footfalls echo in the dark,
Each step a wandering spark.
Into the depths, the heart will lead,
With courage found in each new seed.

Silent whispers fill the void,
In shadows where hopes are toyed.
Yet through the fear, a flame will rise,
Illuminating hidden skies.

The Allure of What Lies Ahead

A horizon painted in shades unknown,
A song of wanderlust is sown.
Beyond the veil where dreams ignite,
Lies the allure of future's flight.

In every heartbeat, a story begins,
Where laughter dances, and adventure spins.
With open arms, we'll chase the dawn,
Embracing paths as yet unspawned.

Charting the Unexplored

Maps unfurl in the hands of fate,
Lines that twist, and hearts elate.
Where treasures lie in wait unseen,
In realms untouched, we'll dare to dream.

Navigating through the misty trails,
With stars as guides, we'll follow sails.
Each step a brush on the canvas wide,
Charting the unexplored with pride.

Lost in the Labyrinth of Wonder

In a maze where shadows play,
Whispers call from far away.
Every turn a secret keeps,
Where the mind forever leaps.

Winding paths and endless dreams,
Reality is not as it seems.
Colors dance in twilight's glow,
As we wander, risk and flow.

Faint echoes of a laughing child,
Lost within the forest wild.
Curious hearts and searching hands,
Drawn to mysteries of distant lands.

Amidst the twists, we find our way,
Guided by the stars' array.
In the labyrinth, life is spun,
Forever lost, yet always fun.

Treading New Footfalls

Each step forward, a fresh start,
Chasing dreams with an open heart.
Paths unknown, horizons wide,
With every stride, we learn to glide.

Embrace the sun, feel the breeze,
Nature sings, putting minds at ease.
Mountains beckon, rivers flow,
To the places we long to go.

Footfalls echo through the days,
In gentle whispers, life conveys.
New adventures like a song,
Encouraging us to move along.

With courage built on faith and hope,
We tread the path, we learn to cope.
Each footfall a note in life's song,
Creating rhythms where we belong.

The Enchantment of the Unrealized

Unwritten dreams in sleepless night,
Glimmers of vast worlds in sight.
A canvas bare, the colors wait,
For the brush of a heart's fate.

Echoes dance in silent halls,
Magic lingers, softly calls.
Potential wrapped in tender care,
Awaits the soul that's willing to dare.

In the shadows of what could be,
Lie the pathways, wild and free.
Yearning hearts with fiery zeal,
Find the strength to dream and feel.

Unraveled truths in starlit skies,
Boundless realms where wonder lies.
In the whisper of the unrealized,
Lives the magic, yet disguised.

A Glimmer in the Twilight

As daylight fades and shadows rise,
A glimmer shines in quiet skies.
Fleeting moments, soft and rare,
Hold the beauty of despair.

Twilight whispers secrets sweet,
As day and night begin to meet.
Crickets sing, the stars come out,
In stillness, dreams stir without doubt.

A world transformed with softest light,
Beauty glows in every sight.
Hope emerges in the dark,
A gentle flame, a steady spark.

With every breath, we find a way,
In twilight's arms, we choose to stay.
A glimmer here, a chance to see,
That life's embrace is wild and free.

The Singularity of Unfamiliarity

In shadows dance the unknown dreams,
Waves of silence stir the seams.
Unraveled threads, a story untold,
Where whispers linger, mysteries unfold.

Veils of doubt shroud the light,
A canvas blank, cloaked in night.
The pulse of chaos gently beats,
As every heart with wonder greets.

Paths unworn call to the brave,
In the depths, the lost souls pave.
Through fear, we find the hidden truths,
Each step, a leap into the youths.

In stillness, clarity takes flight,
With every breath, we ignite the light.
The singularity awaits our gaze,
As we embrace the unknown ways.

Under the Canopy of Enchantment

Beneath the leaves, a world concealed,
In twilight moments, dreams revealed.
The whispers of the winds do weave,
A tapestry that none conceive.

Stars above in a velvet sea,
To every heart, they hold the key.
The branches sway, a gentle tune,
Guiding souls like the silver moon.

In every shadow, magic breathes,
A symphony that the forest weaves.
Between the roots, secrets hide,
Under the canopy, we confide.

With every step, the spirits dance,
In quiet moments, we find romance.
Embracing wonder's sweet embrace,
In this enchanted, sacred space.

The Sweet Surrender to the Uncharted

Adventurous hearts, let go of fears,
Embrace the path with joyful cheers.
The horizon calls with a siren's song,
In the unknown, we all belong.

With open arms, the journey starts,
A leap of faith ignites the hearts.
Through stormy seas and winding trails,
In the uncharted, the spirit sails.

Tales of travelers, whispers of old,
In every story, courage unfolds.
Take the chance, dive into the deep,
In the unfamiliar, our dreams we keep.

With every turn, we find our way,
In the wild, we learn to play.
The sweet surrender, a cherished gift,
In the unknown, our souls uplift.

Lighthouses in the Void

In darkness stand the towers bright,
Guiding ships through the endless night.
Their beams of hope, a steadfast theme,
In the vastness, they softly beam.

Amidst the storms that howl and scream,
Lighthouses whisper like a dream.
A beacon's call, so strong and clear,
Through raging tides, they persevere.

The void may stretch, a daunting sight,
Yet every heart can find the light.
With anchors set, we sail the sea,
Lighthouses shine, a promise to be.

In solitude, the glow ignites,
Navigating through the darkest nights.
These steadfast souls, with grace, they stand,
In the void, they lend a guiding hand.

Echoes of Forgotten Paths

In the woods where whispers dwell,
Footprints fade, stories tell.
Maps of dreams, a fading chart,
Lost in time, they play their part.

Beneath the leaves, a secret's song,
Each note tells where we belong.
Echoes linger, paths recede,
In every heart, there lies a need.

Memories dance with fluttering grace,
In twilight's arms, we find our place.
Guide us gently, winding ways,
Through the shadows, light will blaze.

History's thread, weaves and spins,
Through silence deep, the journey begins.
Embrace the echoes, hear them call,
In forgotten paths, we're one and all.

Shadows of the Unseen

Beneath the veil of twilight skies,
Lurking doubts and soft goodbyes.
Whispers float on the evening breeze,
Shadows dance among the trees.

Hidden truths and quiet fears,
Memories wrapped in fragile years.
In darkness deep, they find their way,
Guiding hearts that choose to stay.

Glancing back to what we know,
These shadows cast, they ebb and flow.
Their silent stories, always near,
Whisper wisdom, calm our fear.

In the stillness, we're entwined,
The unseen holds what we can't find.
Step with caution, trust the night,
In the shadows, find your light.

Venturing into the Abyss

Into the depths where silence reigns,
A realm unknown, stripped of chains.
Glimmers flicker on the edge of night,
Pulling souls to explore the fright.

Courage blooms in darkest space,
Every heartbeat sets the pace.
Venturing forth with hope in hand,
In the abyss, we take our stand.

Unknown whispers beckon low,
Ancient secrets yearn to grow.
Through the shadows, fears collide,
In the depths, find light inside.

Yet every step, a choice defined,
Face the void, leave doubts behind.
In the abyss, we learn to be,
Brave explorers of the free.

The Call of Hidden Realms

Beyond the hills, where dreams reside,
A call unfolds on the evening tide.
Visions stir in the gathering mist,
In hidden realms, our souls persist.

Flashes of light break the mundane,
Enchanting whispers call our name.
Across the veils, time stands still,
The heart awakens, bends to will.

Mosaics of colors, dancing soft,
In secret gardens, we drift aloft.
Every petal holds a prayer,
In each realm, there's magic to share.

As night descends, we take a leap,
Into the depths, our promise to keep.
The call resounds, a sweet appeal,
In hidden realms, we're free to feel.

Painting with Colors of the Undiscovered

In a canvas bright and wide,
Brushstrokes dance with untamed pride,
Hues of hope and shadows play,
Whispers of night, and dreams of day.

Every color tells a tale,
Of valleys deep and mountains pale,
Where visions grow in fertile ground,
And secrets of the heart are found.

A palette rich, a symphony,
Each shade a note, each tone a key,
In this world where visions blend,
Creativity knows no end.

Underneath the stars so bright,
Art flows freely, pure delight,
With every stroke, the soul takes flight,
In colors bright, there's endless light.

Archways to Ambiguous Worlds

Beneath the arches, shadows dwell,
Echoing stories they long to tell,
Paths uncharted, beckon near,
Whispers of dreams, both lost and clear.

With every step, a choice unfolds,
New horizons, bravery bold,
Mysteries wrap like cloaks around,
In the silence, where hopes abound.

Mirrors reflect what lies within,
Fragments of joy, and shades of sin,
Yet in the maze, we find our way,
Through archways that night turns to day.

The journey twists, the fates align,
In the unknown, our spirits shine,
Each doorway whispers, life imbued,
In ambiguous worlds, we're renewed.

The Mystery of the Untamed

In the wild where shadows roam,
Nature sings, a verdant home,
Mysteries buried in the deep,
Secrets the forest aims to keep.

Echoes of wildlife call and croon,
Under the watchful gaze of the moon,
Every rustle, a story told,
In the embrace of the strong and bold.

Winds carry tales of ancient lore,
Life blooms rich forevermore,
Where untamed hearts learn to fly,
In the wilderness, spirits high.

A dance of chaos, wild and free,
Nature's canvas, pure decree,
In every leaf, a tale retained,
In the mystery of the untamed.

Threads of Adventure Unspooled

In a tapestry winding and grand,
Adventures await, just take my hand,
Threads of stories, woven tight,
A journey begins, igniting the night.

Each twist and turn, a chance to learn,
Beneath the stars, our passions burn,
Through valleys low and mountains high,
In every moment, the spirits fly.

Not all paths lead to the same light,
Some fade away, others ignite,
In laughter shared and tears that fall,
We gather the threads, we hear the call.

With every fabric, dreams unfold,
A tale of courage, forever told,
In the threads of life so richly spun,
Adventure awaits, for everyone.

Shadows of Uncertainty

In the quiet of the night,
Whispers linger, doubts take flight.
Footsteps falter, paths unclear,
Echoes of what we hold dear.

Fingers trace the fading light,
Searching for a spark so bright.
Yet shadows dance within the haze,
Misty thoughts that twist and graze.

Where do we go when hope feels thin?
Lost in the maze of where we've been.
Yet through the gloom, we still must tread,
For paths unknown lie just ahead.

The Lure of Untamed Horizons

Waves crash upon the rugged shore,
A siren's call, we can't ignore.
The horizon glows with promise bright,
Where dreams are forged in endless flight.

Mountains rise, a daring climb,
With every step, we lose track of time.
The wind's sweet song ignites our souls,
As we seek out our untamed goals.

The valleys whisper tales of old,
Of bravery and hearts so bold.
The lure of freedom, wild and vast,
Calls us onward, we'll follow fast.

Unknown Horizons Beckon

Beyond the veil of morning mist,
A call to venture, hard to resist.
With every breath, a chance anew,
The unknown beckons, bright and true.

We stand on cliffs, the world below,
Hearts racing with a thrilling glow.
Dreams unfold like wings in flight,
Embracing change in the fading light.

On distant shores, our spirits roam,
We face the void, yet feel at home.
With courage sewn into our seams,
We chase the fabric of our dreams.

Dances with the Unfamiliar

In twilight's glow, we sway and turn,
With every step, our passions burn.
The melody of chance we hum,
As skies ignite, uncertainty's drum.

Hands entwined with dreams so rare,
We dance through shadows, unaware.
Each twirl reveals a secret door,
To lands unseen, we yearn for more.

Laughter echoes in the dark,
Guiding us to each hidden spark.
As we lose ourselves in this sweet trance,
We find our souls in chance's dance.

The Allure of the Unmapped

In shadows deep where maps dissolve,
The heart ignites, the soul evolves.
With every step on paths unseen,
Adventure waits, a vibrant dream.

Whispers call from distant lands,
The compass spins, yet fate still stands.
Curiosity, a guiding flame,
To seek the wild, not play the game.

Beneath the stars, the heavens sing,
A cosmic dance, a timeless ring.
We wander forth, not lost, but free,
In every choice, our destiny.

We chase the dawn, we greet the night,
Through unmarked trails, we find our light.
In uncharted realms, our spirits soar,
The allure of the unmapped, forevermore.

Embracing the Fear of the Unknown

At the edge where comfort ends,
An uneasy heart, but courage bends.
Fear whispers softly, tales of dread,
Yet the brave will rise, where angels tread.

With trembling hands and a pounding chest,
We face the shadows, we face the quest.
Each uncertainty a stepping stone,
In the depths of fear, our strength is grown.

Through the fog of doubt, we pierce the night,
With each bold move, we claim our right.
Embrace the unknown, let courage gleam,
For in the dark, we find our dream.

So take a breath, let the wild in,
For every loss, new journeys begin.
In the arms of fear, we learn to fight,
And in that struggle, we find our light.

Venturing into the Whispering Wilderness

In forests thick where secrets sleep,
The heartbeats quicken, the shadows creep.
Each rustle speaks a tale untold,
In nature's grasp, we are made bold.

The call of birds, a siren's song,
Through towering trees, we wander strong.
With every step, the earth we claim,
In whispering woods, we stake our name.

Where rivers flow and mountains rise,
In beauty's grip, our spirits fly.
The wilderness calls, a sacred space,
In every leaf, we find our grace.

As twilight falls and stars ignite,
The wild embraces us with its light.
In every breath, we feel it near,
The whispering wilderness, oh so dear.

Echoes from the Depths of Silence

In silence deep, where shadows linger,
The echoes speak, a gentle zinger.
Words unspoken, thoughts that roam,
In quietude, we find our home.

The softest sigh, a fleeting breeze,
In moments still, we drift with ease.
Each heartbeat marks a tale profound,
In the depths of calm, wisdom is found.

The world can roar with chaos loud,
Yet in the hush, we stand unbowed.
With open ears, we heed the call,
In silence, we learn to embrace it all.

So let us dwell where whispers rise,
In tranquil realms beneath the skies.
For in the depths, a clarity shines,
Echoes from silence, forging the lines.

Embracing the Wild Unknown

Whispers of the forest call,
A symphony of rustling leaves,
Footprints wander, wild and free,
Adventure awaits in shadows deep.

Stars twinkle in a velvet sky,
Echoes of laughter ride the breeze,
Nature's heart beats strong and bold,
In every step, new tales unfold.

Mountains rise, majestic and grand,
Rivers carve paths through the land,
With open arms, we greet the night,
In the wild, we find our light.

Embrace the journey, take the chance,
In the wild unknown, let your spirit dance,
For every fear, there's courage to find,
In the unknown, our hearts unwind.

The Mystery Beneath Everyday Sight

The world spins in everyday hues,
Yet hidden truths lie in plain view,
A touch of magic in common things,
Whispers of wonder the morning brings.

Eyes half-closed in the morning light,
The mundane wraps in a cloak of night,
Each step through the day holds a spark,
A soft reminder, there's more in the dark.

Pedestrians pass without a glance,
Unseen stories weave in a dance,
In crowded markets and silent streets,
Mystery lingers, where heartbeats meet.

Beneath the surface, secrets reside,
In every breath, let curiosity guide,
For life's rich tapestry waits to be spun,
In the ordinary, the extraordinary's begun.

Unraveling the Threads of Fate

In the loom of life, threads intertwine,
Stories woven, yours and mine,
Paths cross like rivers in the night,
Destinies dance in the soft twilight.

With every choice, a pattern grows,
In the tapestry of life, it shows,
Threads of joy and sorrow blend,
Unraveling mysteries without end.

A flicker of fate, a sudden pause,
Moments captured without a cause,
In the stillness, a whisper of chance,
Life unfolds in a delicate dance.

Weaving dreams with hands of hope,
Building bridges, learning to cope,
In the fabric of time, we find our place,
Each thread a story, each knot a trace.

Dwelling in Shadows and Secrets

In corners dim, secrets hide,
Whispers echo where dreams reside,
The night unveils what day won't show,
In shadows, the mystery starts to grow.

Behind closed doors, stories unfold,
Tales of the brave and the bold,
In the silence, the heartbeats grow,
Dancing in places few dare to go.

A flickering candle casts a glow,
Revealing the paths we hardly know,
In twilight's embrace, fears come to light,
Secrets linger, hidden from sight.

To dwell in shadows is to explore,
The depths of the soul, forevermore,
In the quiet, our truths we find,
In the folds of darkness, we are entwined.

The Enigma of the Unfamiliar

Whispers dance in the dark,
Shadows murmur secrets vast.
Footsteps tread on unknown paths,
Curiosity grips the heart.

Veils of mist conceal the truth,
Mysteries beckon from afar.
Weaving thoughts of what could be,
Chasing answers like a star.

In silence, echoes call my name,
Voices lost in the night's embrace.
Fear and wonder intertwine,
As I wander through this space.

Each turn reveals a hidden sign,
Faint glimmers spark the mind's delight.
The unfamiliar sings a song,
A gentle pull towards the light.

A Map of Forgotten Places

A crumpled map lies in my hands,
Treasures drawn by ancient hands.
Forgotten towns, lost in dust,
Each mark a tale, a voice it stands.

Rivers twist through silent plains,
Whispers from a time long past.
Lost civilizations fade in dreams,
Yet the memories hold steadfast.

Overgrown paths where stories sleep,
Echoes of laughter, joy, and tears.
Each step leads to a fragment found,
A bridge from silence to our years.

In the heart of silence, I will seek,
The places time forgot to keep.
Unfold the map, take a breath,
Awake the dreams that lie so deep.

The Veiled Route of Discovery

In the fog, a trail unfolds,
Winding through the depths of thought.
Each step upon the hidden way,
Leads to knowledge long sought.

Veiled in layers of passing time,
Wisdom waits with quiet grace.
Secrets buried beneath the stone,
Awaits the brave to find their place.

Echoes whisper through the trees,
Stories wrapped in nature's weave.
The path is fraught with doubts and fears,
Yet onward, we must believe.

With each discovery, a spark ignites,
Illuminating worlds unknown.
Guided by the heart's own light,
In the veiled, we find our home.

Starlit Pathways of Mystery

Beneath the sky, the stars align,
Infinite tales in their glow.
Each twinkling light a guiding spark,
Through the mysteries they bestow.

Night whispers secrets to the brave,
As shadows stretch across the land.
Starlit trails beckon the heart,
Inviting dreams to take a stand.

Lost in wonder, I will tread,
On pathways woven with delight.
Each step a dance with cosmic fate,
A journey through the endless night.

In the silence, whispers call,
As galaxies twirl in the deep.
Starlit pathways lead me on,
Where mysteries and dreams still sleep.

Descending into Night's Embrace

The stars blink softly in the dark,
Whispers of silence find their mark.
Shadows dance where moonlight plays,
As dreams unfold through gentle haze.

The cool breeze carries night's sweet song,
In this stillness, where I belong.
The world drifts softly out of sight,
Embraced gently by the night.

A canvas painted black and blue,
Spangled skies with a hint of hue.
Each heartbeat slows, a tranquil sigh,
As twilight's veil cloaks the sky.

With each passing moment, time suspends,
In the darkness, as magic blends.
I close my eyes, let worries cease,
In night's embrace, I find my peace.

The Allure of Untraveled Roads

Winding paths beneath the trees,
Whispers carried by the breeze.
Each step forward, a call to roam,
Leaving behind the comforts of home.

The sun dips low, a golden hue,
With every turn, discoveries new.
Footprints linger, a fleeting trace,
On roads untouched, I find my place.

Curiosity sparks like a fire,
Each journey fuels my heart's desire.
In every moment, adventure blooms,
With every breath, the spirit resumes.

Though maps may guide and signs may lead,
It's the unknown that plants the seed.
With open arms, I greet the bold,
On untraveled roads, the stories unfold.

Sailing the Sea of Enigma

Beneath the waves, where secrets hide,
The ocean's depths are a thrilling ride.
With sails unfurled, I chase the tide,
In a quest for truths that can't abide.

Misty horizons, a ghostly view,
Each wave whispers something new.
Echoes of legends, old and deep,
In the sea's embrace, I sink and leap.

Stars above reflect on the brine,
Navigating dreams through a world divine.
The salt in the air, the wind in my hair,
A sailor's heart beats wild and fair.

Where will the currents take my soul?
In this vast expanse, I've found my role.
Exploring the depths, the call of the sea,
In the sea of enigma, I am free.

The Lure of the Unfathomable

In shadows cast by distant lights,
The unfathomable ignites the nights.
Mysteries swirl like fog through air,
Inviting souls to venture where.

Veils of silence cloak the unknown,
In the cracks of reality, seeds are sown.
What lies beyond the edge of sight,
Awakens whispers of pure delight.

Fingers stretch to touch the obscure,
Eager hearts seek out the allure.
With every question, new paths appear,
In the depths of wonder, there's no fear.

Delve into realms where reason bends,
Embrace the magic that never ends.
With each step, the unknown unfolds,
In the lure of the unfathomable, we're bold.

Embracing the Hidden

In shadows where whispers play,
Truths lie waiting to be found.
Buried deep, they softly sway,
In silence, their echoes resound.

Veils of night, a tender shroud,
Guarding dreams from the light.
In every thought, a voice so loud,
Calling us to take flight.

The heart knows paths unseen,
Guided by invisible hands.
In the quiet, we glean,
Secrets only the soul understands.

With courage, we bring to light,
What the world wishes to hide.
In the dark, we claim our right,
To stand where the truth resides.

Navigating the Nebula

Stars are born in cosmic dance,
A tapestry of dreams and light.
Through the vastness, we take a chance,
Chasing visions through the night.

Galaxies whisper tales untold,
In the shimmer of the cosmic sea.
With each journey, our hearts unfold,
Tracing paths where we long to be.

In swirling mists, we find our way,
Guided by hope's gentle flame.
Every moment, a new display,
In the nebula, we stake our claim.

With every comet's blazing tail,
We embrace the unknown, so bold.
Navigating dreams, we will prevail,
In the universe, our fortunes unfold.

Secrets in the Silence

In soft stillness, truths await,
Hidden deep beneath the veil.
Echoes linger, contemplating fate,
Guarding stories we must unveil.

The quiet hum of ancient lore,
Fills the air with reverent grace.
Listen closely, hearts will soar,
In the hush, we find our place.

With every pause, the world aligns,
Silence speaks, a sacred guide.
Through the void, connection shines,
Leading us where hearts reside.

In gentle whispers, we unearth,
The secrets cherished, deeply sown.
In the silence, we find our worth,
Creating spaces we call home.

Lost Amongst the Stars

In the tapestry of night we roam,
Wandering souls, seeking more.
The universe calls us home,
As dreams of stardust we explore.

Each flicker holds a universe wide,
A story waiting to be told.
In every spark, our hopes collide,
In the cosmos, we are bold.

Through constellations, paths entwine,
Binding hearts in luminous grace.
Amidst the dark, our spirits shine,
Finding solace in the vast space.

Though lost, we are never alone,
For in the stars, together we stand.
With every heartbeat, we are shown,
The beauty of this endless land.

The Call of the Unseen

In shadows deep where secrets dwell,
A whisper calls, a silent bell.
Through veils of night, the heart takes flight,
To realms unknown, where dreams ignite.

The stars align, a cosmic dance,
A chance encounter, a fleeting glance.
With every step, the path unfolds,
In mysteries wrapped, the soul beholds.

Through silent woods, the echoes play,
In hidden corners, night turns to day.
Awakened senses, a world anew,
In the call of the unseen, we pursue.

Through the Mist of Mystery

Through misty veils, the shadows creep,
In silence holds, the secrets keep.
With every breath, the fog entwines,
In the mystery, the heart aligns.

A distant sound, a ghostly tone,
Whispers secrets, in twilight's throne.
Beneath the fog, a story grows,
In the layers, truth arises slow.

The winding path leads far and wide,
Into the depths where illusions bide.
Through the mist, we step with grace,
In search of truths we long embrace.

Echoes of Unfamiliar Shores

On distant shores where tides caress,
Echoes linger, whispering less.
With every wave, a story told,
In salty breeze, the memories unfold.

Footprints fade on sandy trails,
While dreams set sail with whispering gales.
In twilight's hue, the horizon gleams,
Upon the waters of lost dreams.

The cultures blend, the voices rise,
In harmony, beneath vast skies.
Through echoes of an unknown land,
We find connections, hand in hand.

Wandering Beyond Familiarity

In search of paths less traveled by,
We wander far where spirits fly.
Each step a chance to learn, to grow,
Beyond the limits of what we know.

The horizons stretch, a canvas wide,
With every turn, the heart's a guide.
In foreign skies, we paint our dreams,
With colors bright, in sunlight's beams.

Beyond the grasp of what is clear,
We chase the mysteries we hold dear.
In wandering souls, the world ignites,
A journey made of endless nights.

Beyond the Veil of Shadows

In the stillness of the night,
Whispers dance along the breeze.
Secrets linger, lost from sight,
Veils conceal what heart believes.

An echo of a distant call,
Promises of the unseen light.
Through the darkness, shadows fall,
Chasing dreams into the night.

In the depths where silence weaves,
Truths unfold like fragile lace.
Beyond the veil, the heart retrieves,
A sacred, forgotten place.

Embrace the fear, let it rise,
For in shadows, courage grows.
Beyond the veil, the spirit flies,
Into the light where love bestows.

Uncharted Dreams Await

In the canvas of the mind,
Colors swirl like painted skies.
Boundless worlds for hearts to find,
Where every moment never dies.

Nestled deep in thought's embrace,
Wonders whisper on the wind.
Adventures spark with every trace,
As the new and old rescind.

Through the gates of time we roam,
Each dream holds a hidden key.
In the unknown, we build our home,
With courage as our guiding tree.

Let the stars be our guideposts,
As we voyage into the night.
Uncharted dreams, the heart hosts,
Where hopes awaken into flight.

The Path Less Traveled

Along the road, the wildflowers bloom,
A journey where few dare to tread.
Hidden gems in nature's loom,
Await the souls who seek instead.

With each step, the fears dissolve,
Unraveling the tightly spun.
In uncertainty, we evolve,
A tapestry of battles won.

Through tangled woods and whispered streams,
A compass forged by heart's desire.
The path ignites our vivid dreams,
As we walk through the thickets of fire.

With every choice, the road expands,
A symphony of fate and chance.
The world awaits in open hands,
On the path where hearts advance.

Whispers of the Abyss

In the echoes of the night,
Voices murmur from the deep.
A siren's song, a haunting plight,
Where shadows gather, secrets sleep.

Through waters dark, the silence breathes,
Promises hidden in the tide.
Beneath the waves, the heart believes,
In depths where longing cannot hide.

The abyss calls with tender grace,
Pulling dreams 'neath the moon's sway.
In the void, we find our place,
A fragile hope that lights the way.

As we drift in darkness' fold,
Whispers guide us to the shore.
In the abyss, our hearts behold,
The promise of forevermore.

Sailing Beyond Familiar Waters

The sails unfurl in morning light,
We drift away from all we know.
The ocean calls, a vast invite,
To chase the dreams where currents flow.

With stars as guides, we'll find our way,
Through tempest winds and tranquil seas.
Adventure beckons, come what may,
We'll dance with tides and ride the breeze.

Each wave whispers tales of old,
Of journeys made and love once lost.
In salt and spray, our hearts grow bold,
Embracing freedom, no matter the cost.

This path is ours, we claim the night,
With every heartbeat, fears untwine.
Sailing beyond, in sheer delight,
A world awaits that's purely divine.

The Grasp of Uncertainty

In shadows cast by fleeting light,
We wander paths where answers hide.
Each step we take, a whispered fright,
Yet hope ignites within our stride.

The choices loom like stormy skies,
With raindrops laced with doubts untold.
But in the dark, a spirit flies,
Embracing all that we behold.

We hold the tension, pulse alive,
Navigating through the haze of doubt.
To thrive in chaos, we must strive,
And find the strength to turn about.

In every twist, a chance to see,
The beauty in what lies unknown.
With courage strong, we forge and free,
Our paths to walk, our truth now shown.

Awakening the Undiscovered Heart

Beneath the surface, beats a soul,
Unseen, unheard, yet full of grace.
In silence deep, we seek the whole,
To find the light in every space.

A gentle touch, a healing song,
Unlocks the doors to dreams once sealed.
The pulse of life, steady and strong,
Reveals the power we concealed.

In gardens lush, where shadows play,
We nurture love, let blossoms twine.
With trust, we open night to day,
Awakening hearts, forever aligned.

Embrace the whispers, soft and clear,
For every heartbeat tells a part.
In love's embrace, we cast our fear,
Awakening the undiscovered heart.

The Journey of the Brave

With compass set and spirits high,
We venture forth, our tales unfold.
Through mountains steep, beneath the sky,
The heart of courage, fierce and bold.

In darkest nights, our lanterns glow,
Illuminating paths of dreams.
With every challenge, strength will flow,
As hope and grit become our themes.

Together bound, we face the storm,
With laughter fierce and spirits bright.
In unity, we shall transform,
The journey's trials into light.

So onward, friends, with hearts ablaze,
We carve our names in sands of time.
For every step in freedom's gaze,
Proclaims our truth, our life, our rhyme.

Embracing the Unfamiliar

In shadows deep, we take a step,
With hearts aflame, we dare to leap.
The unknown calls, a siren's song,
Through doors ajar, where we belong.

With eyes wide open, we seek the light,
In every corner, fear takes flight.
The road ahead may twist and turn,
Yet in this journey, hearts will yearn.

Each new face, a story shared,
With every breath, we've boldly dared.
Together we rise, through trials and pain,
In the unfamiliar, we break the chain.

So greet the dawn with an eager heart,
For each new path is a brand new start.
Embracing change, we'll find our way,
Through the labyrinth of night to day.

Navigating the Endless Night

Stars like whispers guide our quest,
Through velvet skies where dreams rest.
The moon hangs low, a silver thread,
Casting glow on the doubts we shed.

With every step, the shadows creep,
Yet in the dark, our courage leaps.
A compass forged from hopes anew,
Navigating, we push on through.

The winds may howl, the path unclear,
But in our hearts, we hold what's dear.
Together, we'll weather the storm's fierce bite,
Finding strength in the endless night.

As dawn approaches, shadows wane,
The trials faced are not in vain.
In darkness, light finds its place,
Illuminating time and space.

Chasing Dreams in the Dark

When silence falls, and shadows grow,
We chase the dreams we long to know.
In whispered hopes, we find our flame,
Igniting passion, we stake our claim.

Through winding paths, elusive and deep,
In the stillness, we make our leap.
From starlit skies to hidden trees,
We chase our dreams upon the breeze.

The night may cloak our daring flight,
Yet in the dark, we find our light.
With every heartbeat, we stake our claim,
Chasing dreams, we call their name.

So run with purpose, hearts on fire,
For every dream fuels our desire.
In the dark, we truly see,
The boundless spirit we can be.

The Secrets of Unexplored Destinies

Beneath the surface, whispers lie,
In every heartbeat, secrets sigh.
With courage deep, we dare to seek,
The paths untraveled, the future bleak.

Each twist and turn, a lesson learned,
From every moment, wisdom earned.
The horizon beckons with tales untold,
Of dreams we weave, of fates we hold.

In hidden realms where shadows blend,
We find the means to rise and mend.
Unexplored destinies, an open door,
Inviting us to seek and soar.

So gather strength, hold tightly fast,
For every journey shapes our past.
In secrets held, our spirits twine,
The mystery unfolds, our lives align.

Breaking the Boundaries of Safety

In the cradle of comfort, we dwell,
But whispers of danger begin to swell.
Every step forward, a dance with fate,
Caught in the balance, we hesitate.

Yet courage ignites, a flame within,
To stretch beyond walls, the thrill of the spin.
We break through the barriers, bold and strong,
In the face of uncertainty, we belong.

With each risk taken, the heart beats loud,
A symphony of freedom that draws in the crowd.
No longer confined by the chains of fear,
We embrace the unknown, the path is clear.

In the journey of life, we find our way,
Through shadows and doubts, we will not sway.
Together we rise, unchained and free,
Breaking the boundaries, just you and me.

In the Realm of Speculation

In the depths of thought, where ideas take flight,
Imagination wanders, chasing the light.
Questions like stars in a velvety sky,
Spark the desire to know and to pry.

What if the world is not as it seems?
What lies beneath our surface dreams?
In whispers of wonder, we ponder and muse,
Seeking the truth in the shades of our views.

Possibilities dance like shadows at dusk,
Each theory a treasure, each guess a must.
With minds wide open, we weave and we spin,
Unraveling the threads of the possible grin.

Though answers elude in the labyrinth's maze,
Each step we take sparks curiosity's blaze.
In the realm of speculation, we chase the unknown,
Building our visions, together alone.

The Quest for Hidden Truths

In the silence of night, secrets reside,
A quest for the truths that the heart tries to hide.
Through valleys of shadow, we wander and seek,
The echoes of whispers, the silence we speak.

With each clue uncovered, stories unfold,
Layers of time, both poignant and bold.
We navigate paths lined with doubt and despair,
Yet hope lights the way, leading us there.

In the chasms of memory, we search for our past,
The pieces of puzzles, too precious to cast.
Grasping the fragments, we stitch them anew,
In the fabric of knowledge, we find what is true.

As we delve into depths, both perilous and grand,
The quest for the hidden truths makes us understand.
For knowledge revealed is a treasure to hold,
A light in the darkness, a story retold.

Shedding Light on Shadowed Pathways

In corners neglected, where shadows conceal,
We venture with courage, prepared to reveal.
Through alleys of doubt, we walk with intent,
In search of the brilliance that darkness has spent.

With lanterns of wisdom, we pierce through the night,
Illuminating paths that were hidden from sight.
Each step we uncover a piece of our way,
Transforming the night into bright hues of day.

The journey unveils what was once out of reach,
Enlightenment beckons, our hearts it will teach.
Through trials and triumphs, we learn to embrace,
The beauty in shadows, the dance of our grace.

So let us walk boldly, hand in hand we stride,
With light in our hearts, and our fears set aside.
Shedding the darkness, we rise and ascend,
On shadowed pathways, new journeys begin.

In the Embrace of the Uncharted

Waves whisper secrets to the shore,
Stars above guide us evermore.
Paths unknown beckon with a song,
In the embrace where we belong.

With every step, the world unfolds,
Tales of wonders, rich and bold.
Hearts entwined in nature's dance,
Lost in the sway of sweet romance.

Mountains rise like ancient dreams,
Rivers flow with silver streams.
In the wild, we find our fate,
Embraced by love, we celebrate.

Through the mist, new horizons gleam,
Together we chase the wildest dream.
In the embrace of the uncharted,
A journey begun, never parted.

Heartbeats of Distant Realms

Beneath the night, the cosmos glows,
Echoes whisper where silence flows.
Each heartbeat speaks of paths unseen,
Threads connecting worlds between.

Winds carry tales from lands afar,
Stories born beneath the stars.
In shadows deep, our spirits soar,
Heartbeats echo, forevermore.

Across the void, our dreams entwine,
In the fabric of the divine.
Let the rhythm guide our way,
Through distant realms, we choose to play.

In twilight's dance, we find the key,
Unlocking doors to mystery.
With every pulse, we come alive,
In heartbeats, our souls survive.

The Color of Mystery

Whispers painted on the breeze,
Shades of twilight, secrets tease.
In every hue, a story glows,
The color of mystery softly flows.

Crimson passions, emerald dreams,
Velvet shadows in silver beams.
Brushstrokes weave the fabric of night,
In colors deep, we find our light.

Through the veil of the unknown,
In vivid realms, our spirits flown.
With each shade, whispers entwine,
The color of mystery, yours and mine.

Facets of life in brilliant displays,
Unraveling truths in countless ways.
As we dance in the twilight's embrace,
In colors rich, we find our place.

Journeying Through Unfamiliar Landscapes

Under skies of shifting light,
We chart our course in the deep night.
Mountains loom, valleys spread wide,
In unfamiliar landscapes, we will glide.

The earth beneath, alive with sound,
Every step, a treasure found.
Through tangled paths and fields of gold,
Embrace the stories waiting to be told.

Ancient trees whispering grace,
In the wild, we find our pace.
With open hearts, we wander free,
In unfamiliar landscapes, you and me.

As horizons shift to shapes unknown,
Together, let our spirits be grown.
In the journey, the beauty lies,
In every moment, under vast skies.

Treading Untrodden Paths

With every step, the ground feels new,
The whispers of adventure call me through.
Unseen horizons spark my soul's delight,
I wander boldly, day melts into night.

Fields of shadows, secrets hide away,
I chase the dreams that beckon me to play.
The unknown beckons, paths begin to show,
I tread where few have dared to go.

In silence, echoes of the brave resound,
I gather courage as my feet touch ground.
Each footprint writes a story, fresh and bright,
In every turn, I glimpse the morning light.

With heart as compass, I embrace the roam,
These untrodden paths lead me to my home.
In the vast unknown, my spirit is free,
Treading where the heart dares to decree.

Beyond the Frontiers of Fear

In shadows deep, where doubts begin to grow,
The heart convenes to challenge all we know.
With steps of strength, we face the endless night,
Beyond the frontiers, faith ignites the fight.

The fears like mountains loom, yet I will stand,
With courage etched in every trembling hand.
Through storms of worry, hope can light the way,
We forge ahead, into the new day.

In whispered dreams, resilience starts to sing,
Through every trial, boldness takes its wing.
Together we rise, we shatter the glass,
Beyond the frontiers, we move, we amass.

In unity, our spirits weave a thread,
Through valleys low, where others fear to tread.
I hold your hand, no distance shall we fear,
Together we face the world, strong and clear.

The Siren Song of Tomorrow

In twilight's glow, the future whispers near,
A siren's song, both haunting and so clear.
It calls me forward, beckons from the dawn,
To dance with dreams where shadows have been drawn.

With every note, my spirit begins to soar,
The melody ignites the heart's explore.
A canvas blank, both vibrant and untamed,
Tomorrow's promise waits, unclaimed, unnamed.

The echoes linger, guiding through the dark,
In visions bright, I glimpse a hopeful spark.
Each breath a story, each heartbeat a chance,
To join the song, in life's eternal dance.

So, let the music play, let futures blend,
In every note, a journey without end.
With open hearts, we sing of what could be,
The siren song of tomorrow calls to me.

Threads of the Invisible

In the quiet space where silence weaves,
Threads of the invisible, the heart believes.
With gentle hands, we stitch the unseen ties,
Connecting souls beneath the open skies.

The fabric of moments, softly entwined,
In every glance, the sacred is defined.
Through laughter shared and sorrows expressed,
Invisible threads bind us, love confessed.

Each step we take, a tapestry unfolds,
Stories of courage and warmth in woven folds.
The unseen bonds that time cannot erase,
We hold them close in this cherished place.

So let us cherish what the eye can't see,
The threads of life that weave you here with me.
In every heartbeat, love's design is cast,
Threads of the invisible, forever vast.

The Siren's Call of Adventure

In the mist, a voice does sing,
Calling forth the brave and bold.
Waves are crashing, hearts take wing,
Adventures wait, stories unfold.

Secrets hidden in the deep,
Treasures lost beneath the foam.
Daring souls, wake from your sleep,
Rise and seek your ocean home.

Whispers beckon from afar,
Guiding ships to rugged shores.
With the wind they drift like stars,
To the lands of ancient lore.

Onward now, the journey's set,
To the edge of wild and free.
Regret is not a thing to fret,
Adventure calls—come sail with me.

Secrets Beneath the Surface

Beneath the waves, a world awaits,
Mysteries wrapped in ocean blue.
Silent tales of ancient fates,
A hidden realm where dreams come true.

Fish that shimmer, shadows glide,
Life unseen by those on land.
In the depths, where secrets hide,
Magic dances, soft and grand.

Coral gardens brightly bloom,
Whispers from the ocean's heart.
In the silence, there's a room,
For every soul to play a part.

Dive within, lose track of time,
In the depths, let spirits soar.
With each breath, embrace the rhyme,
Of secrets waiting to explore.

A Song for the Untraced Steps

In the meadow, silence sings,
Footprints lost in fragrant grass.
Each step whispers, gently brings,
Stories hidden, time will pass.

Shadows flicker in the light,
Paths not walked, yet calling near.
A melody of day and night,
Sings of journeys free from fear.

Hearts racing on the trails unknown,
Where the wildflowers sway and bend.
Through the forest, time is sown,
In each corner, tales extend.

Listen close, the earth recites,
A song for all who dare to roam.
In every step, the world ignites,
The path you choose can lead you home.

The Trail of the Unseen Stars

Beneath the cloak of night so dark,
Stars are glimmering, soft and bright.
Each one holds a subtle spark,
Whispering dreams, guiding light.

Wanderers tread on paths unshown,
Following the glow so far.
In the silence, seeds are sown,
To find their place among the stars.

Galaxies swirl in cosmic dance,
Stories written in the sky.
Each twinkling light a fleeting chance,
To reach for more and learn to fly.

So take a step, embrace the night,
Trust the journey through the haze.
For in the dark, there shines a light,
That guides each heart through endless ways.

Dreams Danced in the Twilight

In twilight's embrace, we whisper soft,
As dreams take flight, they soar aloft.
Stars awaken, glimmer and gleam,
Painting the sky with a silvery dream.

The moonlight bathes the world in glow,
Each heartbeat syncs with the night's flow.
We chase the echoes of wishes made,
In the realm where shadows and hopes parade.

Numbered wishes, the heart's delight,
Spun like gossamer threads of light.
Awake, we wander in playful chase,
Through the corridors of time and space.

As dawn beckons with golden rays,
We hold in our hearts these twilight days.
For dreams once danced in that fleeting night,
Now flicker softly, holding us tight.

The Quest of the Brave Voyager

Upon the horizon, a ship sets sail,
Guided by stars, unfazed by the gale.
With maps that whisper of lands untold,
The brave voyager dares to be bold.

Through tempest and calm, the voyage begins,
Each wave a challenge, each gust a grin.
With courage as armor, dreams as the guide,
The heart of an adventurer, untried.

Islands of wonder, treasures to find,
In the depths of the sea, where the lost are blind.
A compass of hope, the winds at his back,
On this quest, none will stand in his track.

Returning with tales of glory and might,
The brave voyager emerges from night.
With stories of courage and trials faced,
In the annals of time, forever embraced.

Nurturing the Seeds of Exploration

In the soil of dreams, we plant our needs,
Nurturing hopes, like delicate seeds.
With hands in the earth, we feel the spark,
Each tiny sprout lights up the dark.

Through oceans of questions, we sail anew,
Curiosity's fire ignites the view.
With every journey, a lesson learned,
In the garden of wisdom, passion burned.

From mountains high to valleys low,
With each step forward, our spirits grow.
We map the stars, we trace the seas,
In the quest for answers, we seek our keys.

As seasons change, our dreams will bloom,
In the heart of exploration, there's always room.
Nurturing seeds with patience and care,
Encouraging visions to take to the air.

Shadows of Forgotten Stories

In corners hidden, whispers collide,
Shadows gather, where secrets abide.
Forgotten tales weave through the air,
Of lives once lived, of dreams laid bare.

The echoes linger on dusty shelves,
Memories trapped within stories themselves.
Fragments of laughter, traces of pain,
In the silence, their whispers remain.

Each shadow dances with tales untold,
Of dreams that flourished and hearts turned cold.
In the dusk of time, the stories blend,
A tapestry woven, where all shadows mend.

Let us honor the voices long past,
In shadows and light, their legacies last.
For every story, a spirit that roams,
In the dance of the shadows, their essence finds homes.

Wandering the Mysterious Frontier

In shadows deep, where whispers dwell,
A path unfolds, a tale to tell.
Upon the brink of something vast,
We tread the line where dreams are cast.

With every step, the world shall shift,
A fleeting moment, a precious gift.
The stars above begin to gleam,
As we embrace the silent dream.

Through rugged lands and skies of gray,
We forge ahead, come what may.
The winds of change begin to wail,
In every heart, a daring sail.

So take my hand, let's journey far,
Together we chase the morning star.
For in this dance of fate and chance,
We find our truth in shadows' dance.

Through the Fog of Uncertainty

The mist rolls in, a shroud so thick,
Each step we take feels like a trick.
Yet beyond the haze, hope flickers bright,
Guiding our souls through the endless night.

Questions linger in the swirling air,
What lies ahead, is it despair?
Yet forward we move, bold and free,
Trusting the winds to lead our plea.

Each heartbeat whispers, "Stay the course,"
In every shadow, a hidden force.
Through doubts and fears, we'll surely find,
The strength within our doubting mind.

So let the fog envelop our way,
For in the unknown, we find our play.
Together we brave the cloak of gray,
With hearts aglow, we face the day.

Dance of the Untamed Spirit

In wild embrace, the night ignites,
A fusion of dreams, where passion bites.
With every leap, the cosmos swirls,
As ancient songs of freedom twirls.

The moonlit floor becomes our stage,
As spirits soar, unbound by cage.
In this wild rhythm, we find our voice,
Each note a promise, a daring choice.

With bare feet kissed by nature's breath,
We dance to life, defying death.
Through fire and breeze, we claim our right,
To celebrate through day and night.

So twirl with me, let worries fade,
In every spin, our truth cascades.
Together we weave a tale profound,
In this untamed spirit, we are found.

On the Edge of Mystery

At twilight's edge, where shadows play,
Secrets linger, poised to sway.
With bated breath, we hold our ground,
A fragile thread where dreams abound.

Curiosity ignites the air,
What lies within the depths of care?
To step beyond the known terrain,
In search of whispers, shadowed gain.

Each glance reveals a world untold,
A tapestry of secrets bold.
With hearts aflame, we choose to dare,
To wander through the whispered air.

So join me here, on mystery's brink,
Where hopes collide and spirits sync.
Together, we'll unmask each hidden plea,
On the edge of what is yet to be.

Into the Abyss of Possibility

In shadows deep, we dare to tread,
Where whispers float, and dreams are fed.
A canvas vast, with colors bright,
Awakens hope in darkest night.

Through veils of doubt, we find our way,
In silent echoes, we choose to stay.
Each step a chance, a fleeting spark,
Lighting paths through unknown dark.

The anchor of fear begins to fray,
As courage blooms to seize the day.
Into the depths, we plunge and dive,
In this abyss, we feel alive.

For every turn, a tale unfolds,
In realms of wonder, beauty molds.
The heart expands, the spirit sings,
In possibility, we find our wings.

Horizons of the Unfamiliar

Beyond the hills, where whispers play,
Lie lands unknown, in bright array.
With every dawn, the light unfolds,
A story new, a tale retold.

The canvas of the sky is vast,
With colors fresh that hold us fast.
In curious eyes, horizons gleam,
Awakening the deepest dream.

Venturing forth, we feel the pull,
Of mysteries rich, our hearts are full.
Each step we take, the world expands,
In the grasp of time, we make our stands.

The unknown calls, a siren's song,
Drawing us forth, where we belong.
In every breath, the magic swells,
As we chase dreams, the heart compels.

A Journey Through Eclipsed Dreams

In shadows cast by fleeting time,
Our dreams eclipse, a silent rhyme.
Through starlit paths, we weave our way,
In hopes revived with each new day.

The night's embrace, a soothing balm,
Where fractured hopes find solace calm.
In every star, a wish concealed,
A promise made, a fate revealed.

With every pulse, the darkness wanes,
As courage grows and hope remains.
Through veils of doubt, we rise and soar,
In eclipsed dreams, the heart's encore.

Awaking from the shadows deep,
We find the strength to laugh and weep.
With every dawn, a fresh new start,
A journey forged within the heart.

Faces of a Hidden World

In tangled woods, where secrets hide,
In murmured tales, the shadows bide.
With every step, the past unfolds,
Revealing truths that time withholds.

Each whispered breath, a ghostly sound,
In echoes lost, the heart is found.
The faces change, yet remain true,
In every heart, a hidden view.

Through twilight's haze, we seek to see,
The layers deep that set us free.
In every glance, a story told,
The warmth of dreams in colors bold.

From silent depths, the world will rise,
In hidden realms, beyond the skies.
With open minds, we'll shed the fears,
To greet the faces formed through years.

Fathoms Below the Surface

In depths where shadows weave and play,
The whispers of the sea softly sway.
Secrets held in currents dark and deep,
Silent tales that the ocean keeps.

Creatures of light dance in the gloom,
Guiding souls through the watery tomb.
Beneath the waves, a world so rare,
With treasures hidden, waiting to share.

Echoes of history in every roll,
The heart of the sea speaks to the soul.
Lost ships and dreams lay interred,
In silence, the stories are stirred.

Each dive a journey, a quest for truth,
In fathoms below, we reclaim our youth.
Amidst the darkness, a spark ignites,
A passion for the deep's endless nights.

Searching for the Unrevealed

In twilight hours, we roam and seek,
For mysteries that the wise dare not speak.
Through ancient forests, under starlit skies,
We chase the shadows where truth often lies.

With every step, the world unfolds,
Whispers of legends in the earth's holds.
Hidden paths weave in and out of sight,
Guiding our hearts toward the unknown light.

In the ruins of time, we search for clues,
To unlock the tales that history brews.
Each moment a chance to discover and feel,
The beauty of life, searching for the unreal.

With eyes wide open, we wander the maze,
In pursuit of the wonders, lost in a haze.
Through valleys of doubt, and hills of despair,
A heart filled with hope finds treasures rare.

The Journey Beyond Familiar Shores

Across the horizon where dreams take flight,
We set our sails to the beckoning light.
With courage as our compass, we chart the seas,
Exploring the wonders, blown by the breeze.

Each wave a story, each tide a chance,
To dance with the unknown in a daring romance.
The world expands as we leave the safe,
In the arms of adventure, our spirits waft.

From rocky cliffs to sandy bays,
We follow the whispers of the ocean's plays.
With every journey, the horizon grows,
Beyond familiar shores, adventure flows.

In sunsets painted with colors divine,
We find our hearts' echo, a rhythm, a line.
For in the vastness, we learn to be free,
The journey beyond is where we truly see.

Treading on Forgotten Spaces

In the hush of twilight, where echoes dwell,
We roam through spaces once silent and fell.
Forgotten paths, overgrown and wild,
Whisper the stories of each dreaming child.

With every step, the past gently breathes,
Revealing the wonders that time weaves.
Ghostly apparitions in the fading light,
Binding us close to the memories bright.

In shadows, we trace the outlines of hope,
With love as our guide, we learn to cope.
The beauty of ruins, a canvas aged,
In every corner, a moment encaged.

As nightfall wraps the world in embrace,
We find solace in this forgotten space.
In the quiet allure, our spirits connect,
Treading on paths where the heart reflects.

Milton Keynes UK
Ingram Content Group UK Ltd.
UKHW022006131124
451149UK00013B/1038